WOMEN IN STEM

WOMEN IN
MEDICINE

by Tammy Gagne

Content Consultant
Conevery Bolton Valencius, PhD
Associate Professor and Undergraduate Program
Director, Department of History
University of Massachusetts Boston

Core Library

An Imprint of Abdo Publishing
abdopublishing.com

abdopublishing.com

Published by Abdo Publishing, a division of ABDO, PO Box 398166, Minneapolis, Minnesota 55439. Copyright © 2017 by Abdo Consulting Group, Inc. International copyrights reserved in all countries. No part of this book may be reproduced in any form without written permission from the publisher. Core Library™ is a trademark and logo of Abdo Publishing.

Printed in the United States of America, North Mankato, Minnesota
032016
092016

THIS BOOK CONTAINS
RECYCLED MATERIALS

Cover Photo: Science Source
Interior Photos: Science Source, 1; Leeds Teaching Hospitals NHS Trust/Science Source, 4; CDC, 7; Brian Kersey/AP Images, 9, 43; Djura Topalov/iStockphoto, 10; AS400 DB/Corbis, 12, 15; Corbis, 18; Red Line Editorial, 19, 37; Pat Levitt/PLOS Biology, 20; David Pickoff/AP Images, 24; Mark Hatfield/iStockphoto, 26; Kevork Djansezian/AP Images, 28; Spencer Sutton/Science Source, 31 (left), 31 (right); Justin Sheely/The Sheridan Press/AP Images, 34; Scott Mason/The Winchester Star/AP Images, 39, 45

Editor: Arnold Ringstad
Series Designer: Laura Polzin

Cataloging-in-Publication Data
Names: Gagne, Tammy, author.
Title: Women in medicine / by Tammy Gagne.
Description: Minneapolis, MN : Abdo Publishing, [2017] | Series: Women in
    STEM | Includes bibliographical references and index.
Identifiers: LCCN 2015960520 | ISBN 9781680782684 (lib. bdg.) |
    ISBN 9781680776799 (ebook)
Subjects: LCSH: Women in medicine--Juvenile literature. | Women physicians--
    Juvenile literature.
Classification: DDC 610--dc23
LC record available at http://lccn.loc.gov/2015960520

CONTENTS

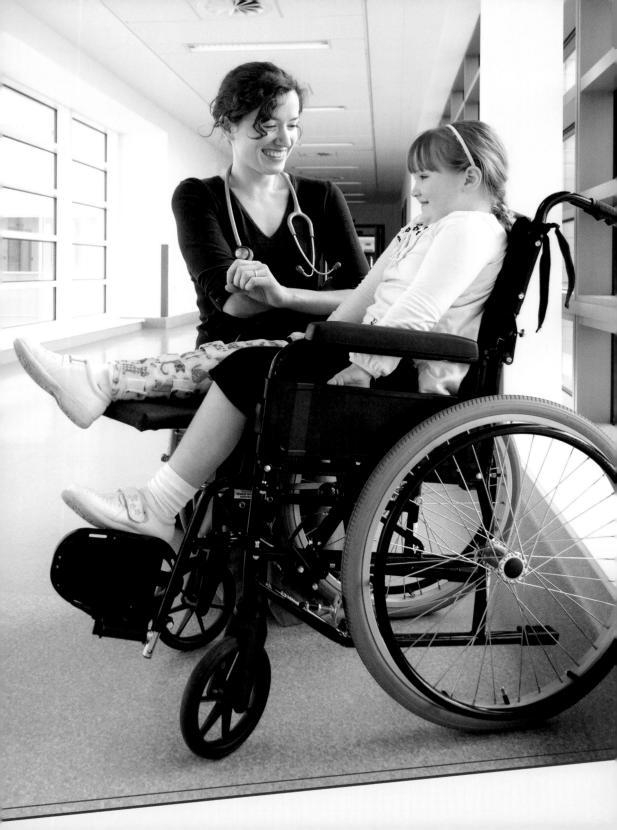

CHAPTER ONE

LIFESAVING WORK

Doctors make a difference every day. Imagine life without them. Strep throat could be life-threatening. A broken leg could leave a person unable to walk for life. Doctors stop small health problems from becoming worse. The world would not be the same without these medical professionals.

Doctors make a big difference in the lives of patients.

Young women can choose from many medical fields. Hundreds of these specialties exist. Some deal with life-threatening diseases. Others involve less serious problems. Some doctors perform surgeries. Others heal with medicines. Medical students might even pursue research. Researchers make new medicines and devices that improve lives.

IN THE REAL WORLD

A Wide Range of Careers

Studying medicine can lead to interesting and unusual careers. Perhaps you would enjoy working as an epidemiologist. These doctors figure out the cause of diseases. They work to prevent those diseases from spreading. Maybe you would prefer being a school psychologist. These doctors study how students develop. Forensic scientists use science and medicine to solve crimes.

Female Doctors and Researchers

In 1930 only about 4.4 percent of doctors in the United States were women. More women have been entering medicine in recent years. In 1952 women earned

In the 1950s, relatively few medical researchers were women.

5 percent of US medical degrees. By 2011 that number rose to 48 percent. After medical school, new doctors enter residencies. This is a period of advanced training. In 2013 and 2014, 46 percent of medical residents were women.

Women are making progress as doctors. But the number of women in teaching and research lags behind. The *Journal of the American Medical Association* did a study about this in 2014. The study looked at medical professors in the United States. Nearly two times more men than women were medical professors. In senior teaching positions, this jumped to almost five men for every woman.

Women in Medicine Month

Each September the American Medical Association sponsors Women in Medicine Month. It honors doctors who have supported women entering the field. Many female physicians have helped forge the path for other women. Many male doctors have also helped open doors for women. They have offered support to students and new doctors. Each of these people has made a difference.

Women also trailed men in receiving research funds. This meant they could perform fewer clinical trials than their male peers. Clinical trials help determine which medicines and procedures are effective and safe.

Despite these challenges, women have made amazing advances in medicine. They have saved lives and kept

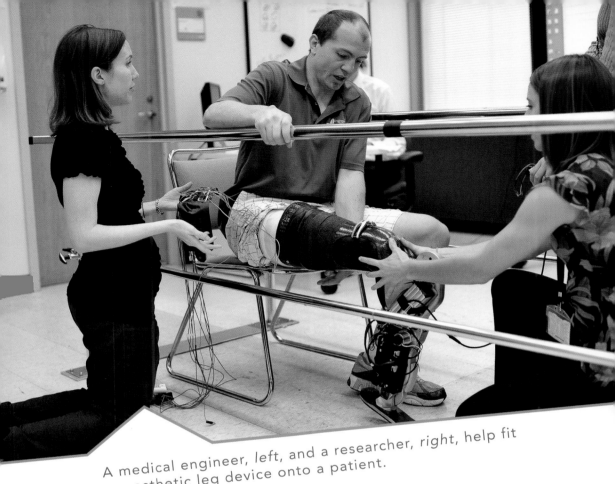

A medical engineer, *left*, and a researcher, *right*, help fit a prosthetic leg device onto a patient.

patients healthy. More women are joining the field today. They will continue to make an impact on medicine in the future.

Why Medicine?

Many young women today are interested in science, technology, engineering, and math (STEM). These

Women are making a difference in every field of medicine, including surgery.

subjects make a good foundation for medical careers. The work can be exciting. Doctors and nurses get to save lives every day. Researchers work to discover cures. Other medical professionals invent incredible devices.

Medical advances help people live longer. When people live longer, they need more health-care services. This means more doctors are needed. The US Bureau of Labor Statistics predicts there will be 123,300 new jobs for physicians by 2022. Many of today's young women will be filling these positions.

FURTHER EVIDENCE

Chapter One contains information about women studying and working in medicine. What was one of the chapter's main points? What evidence was given to support that point? Take a look at the website at the link below. Choose a quote from the website that relates to this chapter. Does this quote support the author's main point? Does it make a new point? Write a few sentences explaining how the quote you found relates to this chapter.

#ILookLikeASurgeon

mycorelibrary.com/women-in-medicine

CHAPTER TWO

BREAKING DOWN BARRIERS

Today many women are doctors or researchers. A century ago, these jobs were rare for women. No good reason existed why women could not study medicine. But the lack of women in the field meant that few women considered it an option. At the same time, many men actively resisted women becoming doctors.

Elizabeth Blackwell was a pioneering female doctor.

Elizabeth Blackwell

Elizabeth Blackwell was born in 1821. She opened doors for later female doctors. Her family moved to the United States from England in 1832. Blackwell's father, Samuel, raised his daughters to believe that they could do anything men could do. This belief inspired Blackwell to apply to medical school. Just getting into a school was a challenge. Schools in Philadelphia, New York, and New England all refused her. She kept applying. Finally, Geneva College in New York approved her application.

Blackwell took advantage of the rare opportunity. She faced many challenges. Her fellow students refused to talk with her. They wouldn't share their notes. Professors made her sit apart from the rest of the class. Blackwell still studied hard. She graduated at the top of her class in 1849. She was the first woman to graduate from a US medical school.

Dr. Blackwell continued to face sexism. Many male doctors would not work with her. Some were

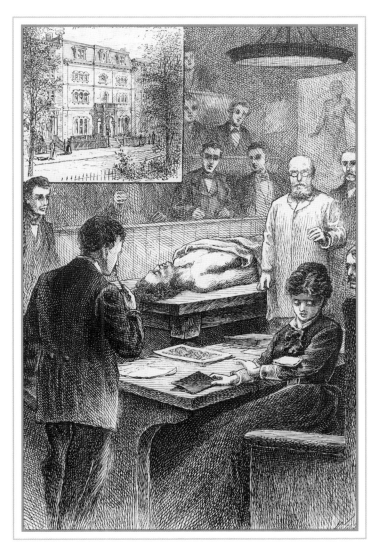

Blackwell faced challenges during her coursework.

hostile. Others ignored her. She did not let them get in her way. She kept working and learning as much as she could. She encouraged her younger sister to study medicine too. In 1857 Dr. Blackwell opened a hospital with two other female doctors. One of the doctors was her sister, Emily. Eleven years later Blackwell opened her own medical school for women.

Baby's First Test

Some doctors become famous for new surgeries or cures. Virginia Apgar is known for something else. She created the Apgar scoring system for newborn babies in 1953. Her method is still in use today. It shows how well a newborn is adjusting to life outside the womb. Doctors use it in the first few minutes after birth. They check such things as pulse, breathing, and movement. The final score can help predict which infants may need more medical help.

Mary Edwards Walker

Mary Edwards Walker picked up where Blackwell left off. Walker was born the same year Blackwell arrived in the United States. Walker's parents encouraged her to pursue her dreams. She wanted to become a surgeon. Walker graduated from Syracuse Medical College in New York in 1855.

Dr. Walker went into private practice and got married. Soon the

American Civil War (1861–1865) broke out. Dr. Walker volunteered to work in a hospital in Washington, DC. Female doctors were still unwelcome in many places. Still, Dr. Walker was able to work as a nurse and a surgeon near the front lines.

Her bravery earned her the Congressional Medal of Honor. She was the first woman to receive the medal. In 1917 the US military reviewed the lists of Medal of Honor winners. It decided some people were not eligible. Dr. Walker was among them. She refused to give up her medal. She was

IN THE REAL WORLD

Top Doc

In 1990 Dr. Antonia Novello became the first female US surgeon general. She was also the first Hispanic person to hold this position. The surgeon general educates the public about health issues. Before taking this role, Dr. Novello worked at the National Institutes of Health. She also helped create laws about organ transplants. This subject was important to her. One of her aunts died of kidney failure. This loss inspired her to specialize in nephrology. This is the study of kidneys.

Walker poses with her Medal of Honor.

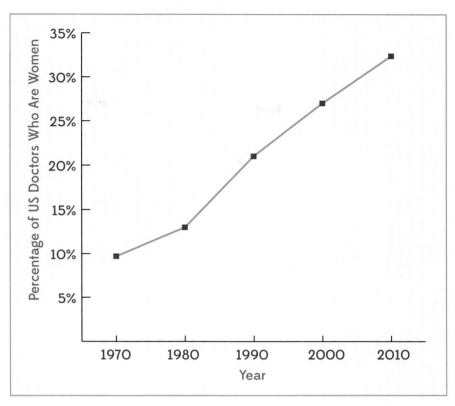

Getting There

Look at this graph of the percentage of female doctors between 1970 and 2010. What do you think Blackwell and Walker would think of this increase? Why do you think the percentage of women still trails that of men? Write about your prediction for the future of female physicians.

proud of her work. Walker was said to have worn the medal for the rest of her life. She died in 1919. In 1977 the US government finally restored the honor.

CHAPTER THREE

ADVANCING MEDICINE

Women have made many important discoveries in medicine. They continue finding new treatments and cures. Some illnesses are not curable. Researchers are learning how to slow them down. This can be the first step to eliminating a disease.

Patricia Goldman-Rakic helped improve our understanding of the brain.

Patricia Goldman-Rakic

Beginning in the 1960s, neuroscientist Patricia Goldman-Rakic researched devastating brain illnesses. Two of these were Alzheimer's disease and Parkinson's disease. Alzheimer's disease causes people to lose memories. Patients eventually forget their family and friends. Parkinson's disease causes people to lose muscle control. Shaking often begins in a person's fingers or hands. It then develops in other parts of the body.

Goldman-Rakic studied a part of the brain called the frontal

IN THE REAL WORLD

Too Much Technology?

Sherry Turkle is a psychologist at the Massachusetts Institute of Technology (MIT). She researches the harmful effects of using too much technology. Computers and other digital devices have improved medicine. But they also lead to people spending less time together. This can result in difficulty interpreting other people's emotions. Turkle hopes her research can help people use digital devices without harming their mental health.

lobe. This has been a difficult region of the brain to understand. Goldman-Rakic mapped brain cells called neurons. Other doctors built on her research to treat Alzheimer's and Parkinson's.

Rosalyn Sussman Yalow

Some scientists work to stop diseases from spreading. Rosalyn Sussman Yalow was one such person.

Many hospital patients lose blood from injuries and operations. Doctors give these people more blood through transfusions. Doctors have performed this life-saving procedure for more than a century. If the blood donor has an illness or other problem, though, it could harm the patient. Yalow helped develop a technique called radioimmunoassay (RIA). This method checks blood for drugs and viruses. It makes blood donation much safer. Yalow's work earned her the Nobel Prize in Physiology or Medicine in 1977.

Yalow poses for a photo just after learning she won the Nobel Prize.

Lydia Villa-Komaroff

People with diabetes cannot produce enough insulin or use it properly. Insulin is a hormone that helps to control a person's blood sugar. Diabetes can lead to serious health issues. It can cause heart problems and kidney disease.

Giving patients insulin was challenging before the 1970s. Doctors used insulin from cows and pigs. Many patients were allergic to these treatments. Human patients needed human insulin. This was where molecular biologist Lydia Villa-Komaroff came in. In 1978 she was on the

Finding the Cause

In 1968 Nancy Wexler's mother was diagnosed with Huntington's disease. This disease damages the brain. Wexler decided to spend her career studying the illness. She looked at genes. These are pieces of information inside cells. Her goal was to locate the gene that caused Huntington's disease. She studied more than 18,000 people with the illness. She succeeded in finding the gene. Wexler is now the president of the Hereditary Disease Foundation. She hopes knowledge about the gene will lead to a treatment for the illness.

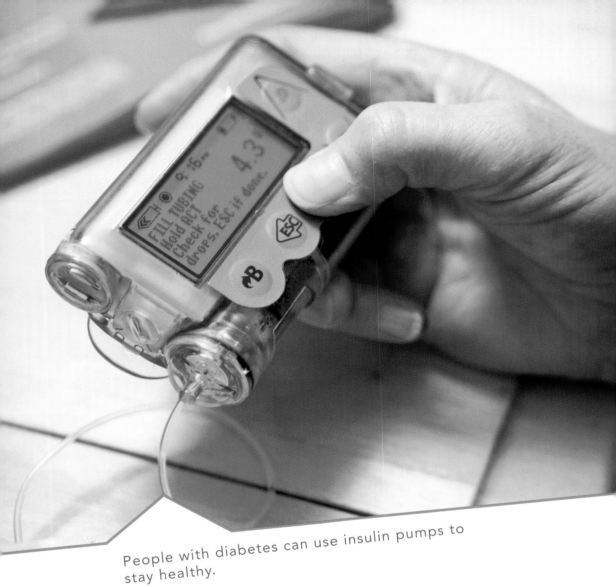

People with diabetes can use insulin pumps to stay healthy.

team that discovered how to make insulin in the lab. People with diabetes finally had a dependable way to manage their illness.

Dr. Mary Susan Fulghum was a resident in the 1970s. She describes what it was like to be the only woman in her program:

> It wasn't 'hard.' I was doing exactly what I had always hoped and dreamed about; I was given this incredible opportunity, and I was always treated with respect, especially by my five fellow male residents, whom I love dearly and always will. We would do anything for each other, to this day. We all worked long, hard hours — we showered and slept in the same on-call room, thankful to catch a few hours sleep in between the ER and the delivery room. I worked as hard as they did — never asked for or was given any special consideration, which was exactly what I wanted. It was an amazing time. I was the envy of my few female general surgical residents because I was treated so well by my boss and fellow residents.
>
> Source: "Interview with Dr. Mary Susan Fulghum." UNC Department of Obstetrics & Gynecology. UNC School of Medicine, 2015. Web. Accessed February 9, 2016.

What's the Big Idea?

Take a close look at Dr. Fulghum's response. What is her main idea? What evidence supports her points? Come up with a few sentences that show how she supported her points with this evidence. How does Dr. Fulghum's experience differ from the experience of Dr. Elizabeth Blackwell?

CHAPTER FOUR

TODAY'S TOP HEALERS

Women continue to change the field of medicine. Female researchers and doctors make a difference in the lives of patients around the world. Their specific fields vary. But they all share a common goal. They work to improve people's health.

For many years Dr. Susan Love has worked to find a cure for breast cancer. This disease strikes about one

Susan Love is a top expert on breast cancer.

in eight US women. Love wanted to become a doctor at an early age. In 1980 she became the first female surgeon at her hospital in Boston, Massachusetts. By 1988 she had founded her own breast cancer center.

Dr. Love has also been a pioneer in educating breast cancer patients. She wrote *Dr. Susan Love's Breast Book*. The book was in its sixth edition by 2016. The *New York Times* called it "the bible for women with breast cancer."

Patricia Bath

Ophthalmologist Patricia Bath's story includes many firsts. In 1975 she

The left image shows normal vision; the right image shows the vision of a person with cataracts.

joined the Jules Stein Eye Institute at the University of California, Los Angeles's School of Medicine. She was the first woman appointed to this position. She became a role model for other women interested in eye health. Her next accomplishment would make her famous.

One of the most common eye problems is a cataract. This cloudy film develops on the lens of the eye. It makes it hard for the patient to see. Over time a person with cataracts can even go blind.

Dr. Bath invented a machine called the Laserphaco Probe in 1986. It removed cataracts and restored the patient's sight. Some of Bath's patients had been blind for 30 years. She finally gave them back their vision with her device.

Susan Lim

Transplanting organs was once the cutting edge of medicine. By 2016 this kind of operation was relatively common. Still, donors can be tough to find. Many organs can only be transplanted immediately after a donor dies. And sometimes donor organs are not matches for the people who need them. Approximately 20 people die each day because they do not have donors.

Leading the Way

Dr. Alice Niragire works at Rwamagana Provincial Hospital in Rwanda. In 2015 she became the first female Rwandan to graduate with a Master's degree in surgery. She didn't see male medical students as a threat. Instead she says they were supportive of her. Niragire encourages other young women to follow in her footsteps. Her advice is to set goals and work hard at achieving them.

Dr. Susan Lim works toward solving these problems. In 1990 she became the first person to perform a successful liver transplant in Asia. She carried out the operation in Singapore. She soon realized that transplanting cells could be a better solution. This type of operation involves less risk to the patient. Instead of entire organs, doctors could replace just the damaged cells. Dr. Lim's research now focuses on fat cells. She uses them to grow heart, liver, and even brain cells. Her work could save the lives of people with many different diseases.

EXPLORE ONLINE

The focus of Chapter Four is female doctors at the top of their fields today. Read the article on the website below. It offers advice for other women interested in medicine. Were you surprised by any of the information in the article? If so, what? Do you feel more or less likely to pursue a career in medicine after reading this piece?

Get Advice for Women Interested in Entering Medicine
mycorelibrary.com/women-in-medicine

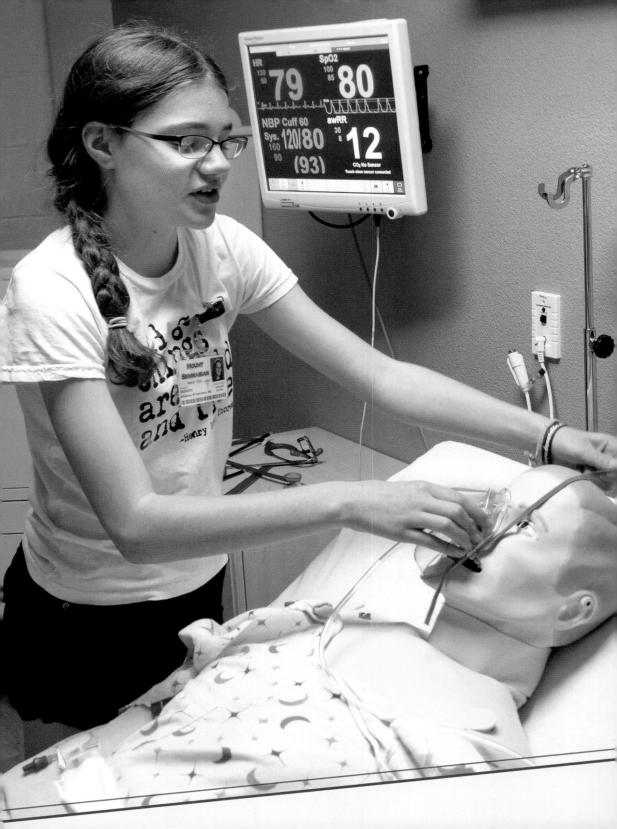

CHAPTER FIVE

YOUNG WOMEN AND THE FUTURE OF MEDICINE

All female doctors today were once young girls considering future careers. For many of them, a career in medicine was an uphill battle. There is still much to discover. New technology creates even more possibilities for research and treatment. Many young women today will become the top doctors of tomorrow.

A fifth-grade student uses a medical dummy to show how to correctly place an oxygen mask on a patient.

Summer Health Experience

The University of California, Irving, offers a program for girls interested in health careers. The Summer Health Experience (SHE) is open to girls 15 to 18. More than 200 girls applied in 2015.

Participants in the SHE program learn about health-care jobs through hands-on activities. The program includes advice on preparing for college. At the end of the program, students take part in a graduation ceremony. Each girl receives a certificate and a letter to include with her college applications.

Awarding Their Accomplishments

The Group on Women in Medicine and Science Leadership Award was created in 1995. This prize honors people and organizations that help advance women in medicine and science. The recipients may be male or female. What matters is that they have played a part in helping women move forward in these fields. Recent winners include Dr. Carrie L. Byington and the Women Scholars Initiative at the Medical University of South Carolina.

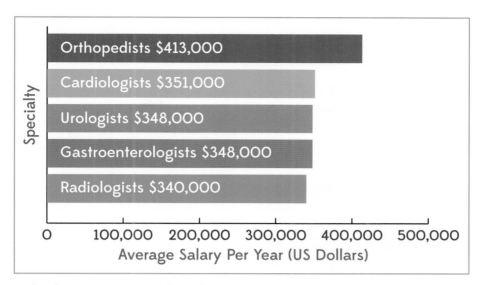

Which Doctors Make the Most?

This graph shows the five highest-paid specialties in medicine. Orthopedists fix bones and muscles. Cardiologists deal with heart problems. Urologists treat problems with the urinary system. Gastroenterologists focus on the stomach and intestines. Radiologists use X-rays to diagnose illnesses. Why do you think these fields pay so well? Write a few sentences about the profession from this list that you find most interesting and why.

Medical Explorers

High school students can learn more through the Medical Explorers Program. This nationwide course allows them to see how a hospital works. Students in this program attend lectures and join group discussions. They also do hands-on projects. Along the way they learn about medicine and community service. Participants meet a few times each month. They learn about surgery and other medical careers.

Stanford Medical Youth Science Program

The Stanford Medical Youth Science Program offers educational experiences for young people interested in medicine. One is for minority students from low-income households. The students in this program stay at the Stanford University campus in northern California. They live there for five weeks during the summer.

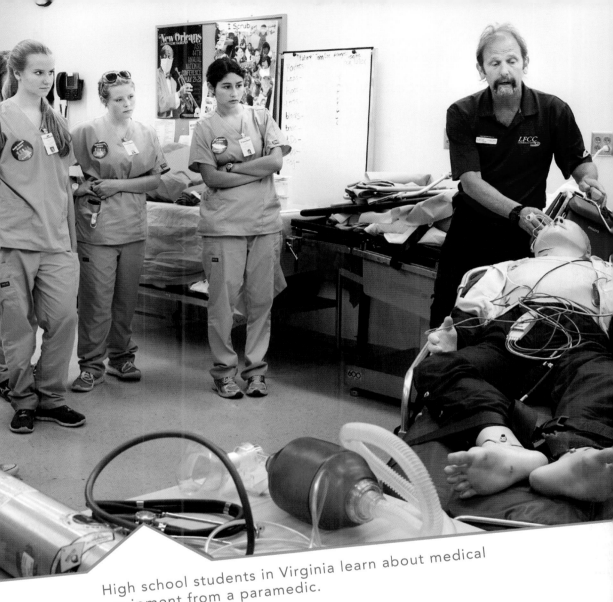

High school students in Virginia learn about medical equipment from a paramedic.

Another workshop runs for three days. Students meet health-care workers from Stanford Hospitals and Clinics. They also get to speak with Stanford students.

The Stanford Medical Youth Science Program has even created a high school course. It teaches students about how living conditions in their neighborhoods can affect health. The program shows young people that medicine is a career that helps people everywhere.

As Dr. Susan Love once stated, "The only difference between a researcher and a patient is a diagnosis." Some young women may be inspired to study medicine to cure an illness that has affected their families. Others might want to become doctors to help people everywhere. They may simply be fascinated with medical science. Whatever their reasons for studying medicine, young women have bright futures ahead of them in these rewarding fields.

Dr. Robin Blackstone knows how discrimination can play a part in the lives and careers of female doctors. She also thinks that women can help one another succeed despite sexism:

> I think the lack of mentoring and support once a woman is hired is still an issue. . . . It is not clear to me . . . that a person who does a math-intensive science versus a different discipline will result in a more gifted physician, teacher, or educator. Many of the sciences that are driving modern medical disease—inflammation, obesity, and diabetes—are not specific to math. Rather, I think that mentoring women in the best way to think through and approach a problem: logic, philosophy, and some of these more 'thinking' sciences may be a more productive fit. In addition, many of the natural skills women have—team building, mentoring, and organizational skills—these tactical skills are very valuable.

> Source: "On the Spot With Colleen Hutchinson: Women in Surgical Leadership —Where Are They?" General Surgery News. General Surgery News, March 26, 2015. Web. Accessed February 9, 2016.

Consider Your Audience

Read Blackstone's advice carefully. Think about how you might explain her thoughts to girls your age. Write a blog post conveying her advice to your fellow female students. How might your text differ from Blackstone's words and why?

Volunteer

Does your local hospital or clinic have a volunteer program? Volunteering is an excellent opportunity to learn about health-care careers. Make sure to ask if you need to be a certain age to volunteer. You may also need to attend an orientation before your first shift. Volunteers may need to commit to a few hours each week.

Interview a Doctor

One way to find out more about what a doctor does on a day-to-day basis is to interview them. Think of some questions you would like to ask a doctor. Then ask your family physician, eye doctor, dentist, or other medical professional if you can interview them.

Research and Write

If you were to become a doctor, what kind of medicine would you practice? Do some research on different specialties and write a paper about what you have learned. You just may discover a new career path.

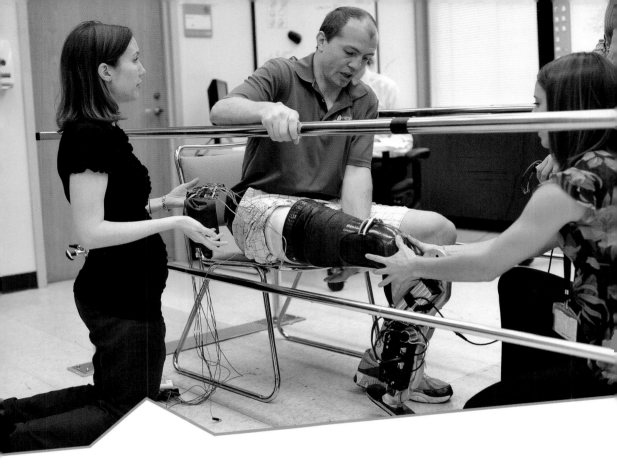

Organize an Event

Many doctors go into medicine because they want to help others. But you don't have to wait until you graduate from medical school to make a difference. Talk to your teachers about planning a blood drive at your school. One of the best ways to help others is getting as many people involved as you can.

Why Do I Care?

Many women have paved the way for other female doctors to enter medical careers. Why is it important for women to support one another in reaching their goals? Make a list of the ways that having another female student to talk to about your interest in medicine would be helpful to you. How do you think you might help her in return?

Tell the Tale

Pretend that you are a doctor on your first day of work in an emergency room. What do you think might be your biggest challenge? Do you think it is difficult to remain calm in the face of an emergency? Write a story about your day. Include information about the different people whose jobs support the doctors in this setting.

Dig Deeper

After reading this book, what questions do you still have about becoming a doctor? Make a list of two or three resources where you might find answers to these questions. They could be books, websites, or people.

You Are There

Imagine you are working with Dr. Mary Edwards Walker near a Civil War battlefield. What are the sights, sounds, and smells of the hospital and the nearby battle? What challenges might the doctors and nurses face? Write a few paragraphs about this experience.

GLOSSARY

discrimination
treating some people better than others for an unfair reason

eligible
qualified to be chosen

inflammation
heat and swelling that results from an illness or injury

mentor
to serve as an advisor or teacher

neuron
a cell in the nervous system

neuroscientist
a person who studies the nervous system

ophthalmologist
a doctor who specializes in eye health

racism
the belief that certain races are better than others

sexism
the belief that one sex is better than the other

transfusion
to transfer into a blood vessel

transplant
to transfer an organ or tissue from one body to another

LEARN MORE

Books

King-Thom, Chung. *Women Pioneers of Medical Research*. Jefferson, NC: McFarland, 2009.

Nordmeyer, Robert. *The Other Side of Courage: The Saga of Elizabeth Blackwell*. Denver, CO: Bygone Era Books, 2015.

Schatz, Kate. *Rad American Women A–Z*. San Francisco, CA: City Lights Publishers, 2015.

Websites

To learn more about Women in STEM, visit **booklinks.abdopublishing.com**. These links are routinely monitored and updated to provide the most current information available.

Visit **mycorelibrary.com** for free additional tools for teachers and students.

INDEX

ABOUT THE AUTHOR

Tammy Gagne has written more than 100 books for both adults and children. She resides in northern New England with her husband and son. One of her favorite pastimes is visiting schools to talk to children about the writing process.